TRAINING AIDS

CONTENTS

CONCEPTS AND CONTROVERSY

AIDS OR GADGETS?

The use of training aids is a controversial subject. Used wrongly, they can undoubtedly cause physical and mental harm but, used correctly – if necessary under supervision from a vet or suitably qualified practitioner – they can help to encourage a horse to move in a balanced way. Training aids can also be utilized to help a horse recovering from injury to use himself correctly and to persuade a horse whose way of going has been spoilt by harsh or ignorant riding that he can work comfortably and correctly.

The important thing to remember is that they are aids to training, not a quick fix for a problem. They are also a means to an end, not an end in itself: whilst some training aids can be used regularly, they should never be thought of as a permanent necessity. If, for instance, you have to ride your horse in an elastic schooling rein all the time, you are compounding a problem, not solving it!

DEFINITIONS

Training aids come in many forms and even basic aids can be valuable: a simple neck strap (which is a training aid for both rider and horse) can be as useful as a lungeing system, and an uncomplicated layout of poles on the ground can help in many ways. There are also training aids to help riders, which in turn will help your horse (see pages 20 and 21). This book introduces equipment and ideas which can help your training and will hopefully encourage you to research training aids and their use further.

PROBLEMS AND CAUSES

Before using a training aid, have an expert assess both you and your horse. Get your riding checked; if you tip forward, for example, you will send your horse on to his forehand. Rider imbalance may be linked to saddle balance and so it is important to get a knowledgeable saddle fitter to check the saddle fit.

If you are in any doubt about whether or not your horse is sound, get veterinary advice because unidentified dental, back and limb problems or foot and/or muscular imbalance can affect a horse's carriage and way of going. It is also important to assess his conformation. Is he physically capable of working in the way you want? Horses with the most unconventional conformation can work beautifully, given time and correct schooling, but only within their physical limits. For instance, a horse who is thick through the jowl will find it more difficult to work in a textbook outline.

A horse may be sound but have uneven muscle build-up. Like us, they may favour one side of the body more than the other, for various reasons. The best way to assess a horse is to watch him working loose wearing no equipment, on the lunge, on long reins and in hand.

BEFORE YOU START

TEN GOLDEN RULES

Before using any training aid, keep in mind the ten golden rules:

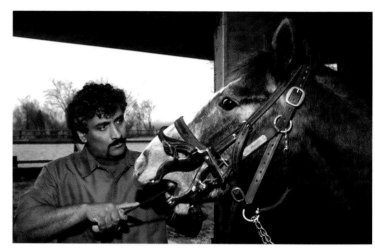

1. Make sure your horse is sound and that his mouth, teeth, back and feet are in good order. This may require qualified, profess-ional advice. If your horse has an established problem and is being rehabilitated (see page 13), work under the supervision of a vet or qualified practitioner. The latter should work with veterinary approval.

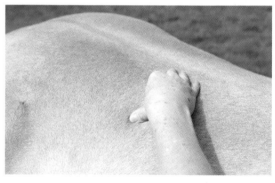

2. Equipment should be introduced carefully and fitted loosely to start with. Even quiet horses can be alarmed by the feel of something different. For instance, some horses are alarmed at first by the feel of long reins or training aids which pass behind the quarters.

3. Check whether equipment is recommended for lunge-ing, riding or both. For example, it is generally accepted that it is not safe to ride a horse fitted with ordinary side reins except when having a lunge lesson.

4. Training aids which attach to the bit should only be used in conjunction with some form of simple snaffle. Do not use a snaffle which employs poll pressure or leverage.

5. If you haven't used a training aid before, try to get advice – and hopefully a demonstration – on its fitting and use by someone who uses it successfully.

6. When you ask a horse to work in a different way, whether with or without a training aid, you are asking him to use different muscles. Only work him for short periods to start with, perhaps only two or three minutes on each rein.

7. Adopting a new posture might lead to slight stiffness and so, unless you are following a veterinary-supervised rehabilitation programme, intersperse work days with relaxation days when you can hack out on a loose rein, turn the horse out to graze, or both.

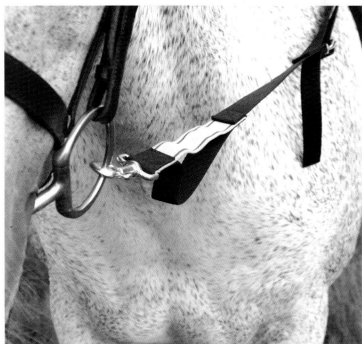

are many pieces of equipment that may influence a horse's head carriage temporarily, but he will only be truly on the bit if he works from behind.

8. Don't expect miracles. A horse can only work correctly if he builds up the correct muscles, which takes time.

9. A training aid only works if it is coupled with correct riding or/and lungeing. There

10. In general, only adults should use training aids designed to influence the way of going on children's ponies. In some cases, children can ride with these aids under expert supervision.

ASK AND REWARD

Results from training, on the ground and under saddle, are achieved by asking and rewarding. First, ask a horse to do something by applying a form of pressure, whether through a leg aid, the reins and bit or a headcollar, and give him time to understand the request. As soon as he responds – for instance, by going forward from the leg, or stopping – reward him by stopping the request and releasing the pressure. Equipment used for leading can work well in conjunction with this principle.

HEADCOLLARS AND HALTERS

Many animals respond well to an ordinary headcollar and lead rope. However, you may need extra help with a strong or 'bargy' horse and something which allows pressure to be applied and released quickly may help as long as the horse is taught to respond to its action. The commonest aids are the pressure halter, the 'horseman's halter' made from thin rope and the nose rope or chain.

A pressure halter may apply pressure on the poll, nose and back of the jaw. A nose rope or chain passes over the front of the nose. There are many commercial designs available, but make sure any equipment you use allows you to release the pressure the instant the horse responds.

ON THE NOSE

Many trainers and practitioners prefer to use headcollars and halters which apply pressure on the nose but not the poll, as they feel that if too much poll pressure is inadvertently applied there is a risk of ligament damage.

You can make a simple nose-pressure system using a check collar designed for large dogs with an ordinary headcollar. Pass the chain through the side rings of the headcollar and across the nose, and then clip a lead rope to both rings.

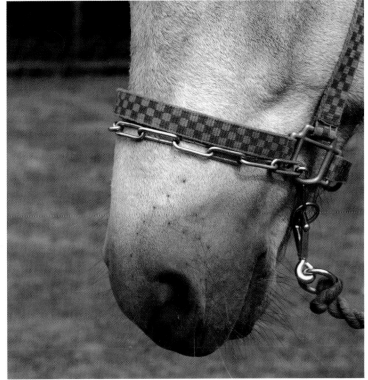

WARNING

Never use any form of pressure halter or pressure headcollar to tie up a horse, either at home or when travelling. If he pulls back and continues to fight, he could be badly injured. **Do not use pressure equipment on foals.**

LUNGEING

Many training aids are for use when lungeing. Some, but not all, can also be used when riding but you should never take risks. Whilst some people ride with side reins fitted, for example, this can be dangerous because the horse may feel too restricted and react violently, possibly causing horse and/or rider to fall. Side reins are fitted for riders' lunge lessons, but the horses and surroundings used are chosen specifically with safety in mind and the instructor lungeing the horse should have the experience and knowledge to be in control.

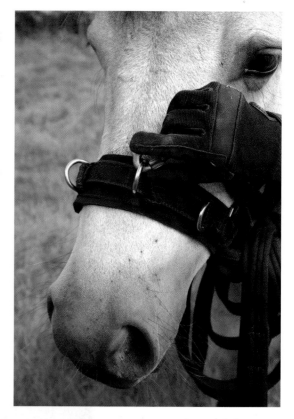

The equipment you use for lungeing depends on the horse's way of going, physical development and what you are trying to achieve. If you are trying to encourage him to accept a light but steady rein contact you might use side reins, but if you are trying to encourage him to stretch his topline, a chambon, EquiAmi or Pessoa may be more suitable. In general, the lunge rein should be attached to the centre ring of a lunge cavesson rather than directly to the bit, to keep communication clearer. Some trainers fasten it to the back ring of a closely fitting headcollar, because they feel a control point on the front of the horse's nose may inhibit forward movement or put him off balance.

SIDE REINS

Standard side reins are a simple way of encouraging a horse to accept the feel of a bit and yield to pressure. They can be made from leather or synthetic materials and be plain, i.e. have no give in them, or incorporate material which allows some give, such as an elastic insert or a rubber ring. Most horses accept the ones with

give, which follow the concept of an elastic contact with the hand, but some trainers feel plain reins encourage a more consistent contact.

Fitting When introducing side reins to a horse who is being backed but who has already been taught to lunge, attach the lunge rein to the centre ring of the cavesson and start with one side rein, attached to a roller ring or the girth at the level of the point of shoulder, and to the cavesson side ring on the outside. If you are starting on the left rein, therefore, the side rein should be fastened to the right-side rings and you will need to change it to the left-side roller and cavesson rings when you change to the right rein. When the horse is happy working with the one side rein, add the second rein. They should be the same length and loose enough for the horse to know they are there without feeling restricted.

The next stage is to attach the side reins to the bit. Again, fit just the outside rein to start with and then progress to the two reins. Start with them loose, but not so loose that they flap and make tiny jerks on the bit, and aim to gradually reach the stage where there is a light contact when the horse has his nose just in front of the vertical.

WARMING UP

Always warm up a horse without any form of training aid. When lungeing, work him briefly on both reins in order to settle him and, when you add the side reins, make any adjustments, such as shortening them, gradually. Most people like to fit protective boots when warming up, especially to shod horses (see page 22).

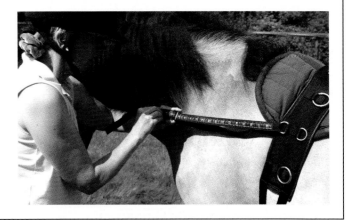

VARIATIONS ON A THEME

Adjusting the height of the side reins can help solve problems but the horse's development and experience must be considered. If he leans on the bit, make sure they are long enough and not too high. If he tends to come above the bit, adjusting them slightly higher may encourage him to work forward to a contact. Some trainers think that crossing side reins at the withers encourages a steady head carriage.

Different types of side reins, or training aids which work on similar principles, may be more suitable for horses who evade the action of standard ones despite correct lungeing technique.

Running side reins are longer than ordinary ones; they pass through the bit rings and fasten to roller rings at different heights on the same side. This allows more lateral flexion because the rein feeds through the bit rings as the horse flexes laterally.

Alternatively, they can be fastened on the roller at the girth between the front legs, then passed through the bit rings and fastened to the roller side rings. This mimics the action of draw reins to some degree, but is not reliant on a rider's quick reaction to release the pressure on the bit (see page 16). As soon as the horse responds by lowering his head and neck, this pressure is released. Some trainers recommend this fitting for horses who habitually come above the bit.

NO ROLLER?

If you don't have a roller, you can use a saddle with the stirrups secured or removed and attach side reins to the girth straps. If you need to lunge a horse and keep control but only have access to his ordinary tack, you can improvise side reins by undoing the centre buckle on the reins and wrapping each half round the girth straps.

WORKING FROM BEHIND

The Pessoa lungeing system, (right) the new EquiAmi training aids and variations of this equipment can be used for routine and remedial work. The Pessoa looks complicated but it is actually simple to fit. It is designed to encourage muscle development from the lumbar region forwards, thus building a topline, and to encourage the horse to work from behind.

The EquiAmi is equally effective and some trainers believe horses are less inclined to try to lean on it, which, owing to its construction, is virtually impossible. Horses must get accustomed to the feel of any training aid in safe surroundings, but this applies particularly to those which pass round the hind legs.

GAITS AND GAIT VARIATIONS

When lungeing and long reining on a circle, trot is the most productive gait in which to build, but control, the horse's energy and make sure he is using his 'engine', i.e. the hindquarters and hind legs. However, with a horse whose basic schooling is in place, you may sometimes want to lunge him in canter to improve the gait.

If you have problems getting a correct strike-off on one rein and are sure it is not due to incorrect riding, lungeing in side reins and adjusting the inside rein a hole or two shorter than the outside one may help. Alter the side reins when you change the rein, or you will be asking the horse to bend the wrong way.

ONE REIN OR TWO?

Lungeing with two reins (sometimes called long reining on a circle) or long reining in straight lines can pay dividends when educating young horses and working those more established in their work. Some people find it hard to handle two reins but practising with an experienced horse and fastening the reins to the side rings of a cavesson rather than the bit to start with will improve dexterity. Most trainers use lunge reins, but others believe leather driving reins or ropes allow more sensitivity: horsemen of

bygone years used rope plough lines when working the field with heavy horses.

THE FEELINE

Trainer Claire Lilley invented the Feeline to make working with two reins on a circle easier. It comprises a single long rein with static and sliding clips that fasten to the bit and roller rings. One rein in effect becomes two that are held as if you are riding from the ground. The

inside rein asks for flexion and the outside one controls the speed. At first, work the horse with the outside rein over his back but as you both become confident and you are achieving the right results, you can bring it behind and around the quarters so that it lies above the hocks. This will encourage him to bring his hind legs under his body.

THE CHAMBON

The chambon is a training device used when lungeing or loose schooling; it is a valuable aid that encourages a horse to lower his head and stretch through his neck and back, minimizing tension. Vets and qualified specialists sometimes use chambons as part of remedial and rehabilitation work. It comprises a pad with rings at each end, which fastens to the bridle headpiece, and a separate part, which fastens to the girth and splits into two cords. These go through the rings on the poll pad, down the side of the face and then clip to the bit rings. It applies gentle pressure to the horse's poll and the bit and, as the horse yields to its action and stretches, the pressure is released.

When introducing the chambon, fasten the clips to the poll pad rings rather than to the bit in order to accustom the horse to the idea of poll pressure. Check that the poll pad is designed correctly, as shown here – some press into the base of the ears, which causes discomfort and irritation.

THE DE GOGUE

The de Gogue is an extension of the chambon system, though not as widely used. There are two fittings: one reacts when the horse responds, whilst the other relies on the rider's expertise and should be used under expert supervision. If you tried to ride in a chambon, there would be a risk of the direct rein confusing its action, but this does not happen with the de Gogue.

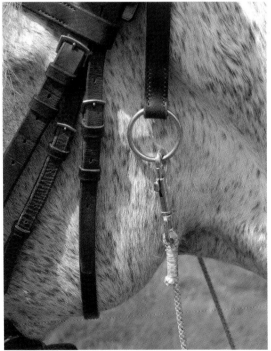

MORE AIDS FOR RIDING

SIMPLY THE BEST

Training aids do not have to be complicated to be effective. Some have become such an accepted part of general riding that they may be regarded as standard tack but, nevertheless, they are still training aids. The basic neck strap is one of the simplest and also most underrated aids.

Fasten a stirrup leather round the horse's neck leaving it just loose enough to lie in the correct place for you to be able to slip your fingers underneath as shown on page 2. When checking the accuracy of your riding in an arena, hold the strap as well as the reins. This helps make sure you use your weight and leg aids when turning rather than relying on the reins. You can then put the same communications into practice when riding normally.

A neck strap is also useful when riding a horse who rushes or runs on to his forehand, or when teaching or reinforcing a half halt. As you signal to the horse to go forward to a slower pace or gait, or to half halt, slide your fingers under the neck strap and give a short pull back, *without* pulling on the reins.

A neck strap is often used to give security to novice riders and prevent them pulling on the horse's mouth when they become insecure. However, it may also encourage them to tip forward and, for this reason, many trainers prefer to use a balance strap (see page 20).

If your horse wears a martingale, you can use its neck strap in a similar way. However, when schooling on the flat in safe surroundings you get a clearer picture of your horse's way of going by removing the martingale and monitoring his movement without it, and using a separate neck strap.

MARTINGALE LOGIC

Many people regard martingales as standard tack but, because they influence the head carriage, they could also be classed as training aids. Whether you use a standing, running or bib martingale, it should be adjusted so that it comes into play when the horse raises his head above the angle of control, not so that it acts all the time. Some trainers like to use a standing martingale on horses who have just been backed because it acts on the nose –

the control point he has been used
to up to this stage – not on the
mouth. A running martingale
acts via the reins and can make
a horse ridden by novice riders,
perhaps in a riding school, more
comfortable by min-imizing
unwanted movements on the reins
and therefore the mouth. A bib
martingale is another form of
running martingale and has the
same action.

A MARTINGALE AND A REIN

The Market Harborough is a
cross between a martingale and a
rein and can help with a horse
who has over-developed muscle
on the underside of the neck by
encouraging him to adopt a better head and
neck posture. It must be fitted so that the
ordinary reins come into a straight-line

contact before the Market Harborough straps
that clip on to them, so that the training aid
only comes into effect when the horse raises
his head too high.

DRAW REINS AND DRAWBACKS

Draw reins and running reins cause more controversy than any other training aids. They have been included here for information but are not recommended for general use because in the wrong hands they can cause physical and perhaps psychological damage. They apply pressure to the poll and rely on the skill and split-second reactions of a rider to release them the instant the horse responds, which takes more skill than many riders realize. How many of us could honestly say we could always apply the right release at the right time, every time?

If the pressure is not released, the horse will not be rewarded for responding correctly and, at best, will be confused. Sensitive horses may show their frustration by running backwards, bucking or attempting to rear.

WHICH IS WHICH?

Although each comprises a single long rein with loops or clips at each end and the terms are often used as if they are interchangeable, draw and running reins are fitted in different ways. Draw reins pass through the bit rings – from inside to outside on one side and from outside to inside on the other, to avoid a pinching action – and fasten to the girth between the front legs. Running reins pass through the bit rings as before and fasten to the girth at the side.

Draw reins apply greater leverage than running reins and ask the horse to lower his head, usually to the point where he is overbent. Running reins ask the horse to bring in his nose but do not draw the head down to the same extent. Some experienced riders say that running reins can be used to help keep a horse straight, but they can also restrict the movement through the shoulder, which is the last thing you want.

USING THE REINS

Both draw and running reins should never be used alone but always with ordinary reins attached to the bit rings. Hold the ordinary reins on the outside of the little fingers and the auxiliary reins between the little fingers and ring fingers, as shown. The ordinary rein with the direct action on the bit should be used first, then, if the horse does not respond, the auxiliary rein. The draw rein must be released immediately the horse accedes to your request.

Draw and running reins will persuade a horse to bring in his nose and, in the case of the former, lower his head and neck. What they *will not* do – and the same applies to all training aids used for riding – is automatically allow you to put the horse on the bit. For a horse to work on the bit, he must have a correctly developed musculature and have reached the stage in his training where he can take more weight on his back end and bring his hind legs underneath him, thus lightening the forehand. This, coupled with acceptance of an elastic contact through the reins to the bit, will bring him to the stage where he can work on the bit, for short periods initially and then, as he becomes more confirmed in his way of going, for longer periods.

Some trainers believe that there are times when using draw and running reins is justified, citing cases where desperate needs call for desperate measures. For example, some people may recommend them for older ex-racehorses who have never been asked to work in a round outline. However, there are other, more subtle training aids that may offer more advantages and fewer drawbacks.

KINDER ALTERNATIVES

STRETCH SOLUTIONS

A training aid must reward the horse immediately he responds to its action. As explained previously, this is why you have to be so careful in the use of draw and running reins, why they should carry the equivalent of a govern-ment health warning and why you should consider alternatives.

As we all aim to ride with an 'elastic contact', it makes sense in many situations to use equipment that incorporates a small amount of give such as the elastic schooling rein, the Lungie Bungie, the EquiAmi mentioned earlier and the FTS Soft Touch.

The elastic schooling rein is simply a long, elastic rope with clips on each end. It passes over the poll, through the bit rings and fastens at the girth either between the front legs or at the sides. When the horse raises his head too high it exerts gentle poll pressure that is released as soon as he lowers his head and neck. As with draw and running reins, the action is more definite when the rein is fastened between the horse's front legs.

The Lungie Bungie does not exert poll pressure and some people prefer it for this reason. Instead, it passes through the ring of a con-necting strap which is fastened to the bit rings and persuades the horse to give to its action through gentle pressure on the bit. Both this and the elastic schooling

rein can be used for riding or lungeing. When riding, aim to keep a similar light but elastic content on the direct rein and whether riding or lungeing, keep the horse working actively from behind.

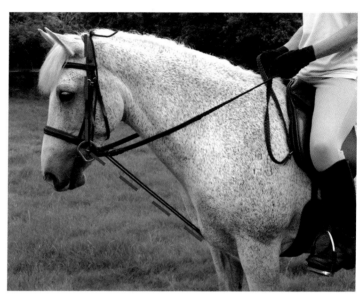

If for some reason you feel neither of these training aids is appropriate, the Barnsby FTS Soft Touch is a more acceptable version of draw reins. It is fitted in the same way as draw reins but a pulley at the girth ensures a less fixed action and minimizes the risk of the horse being forced into an outline. As with draw reins, it should be fitted so that the ordinary rein with the direct action is held on the outside of the little fingers and the training-aid rein between the little fingers and ring fingers, with the auxiliary rein looser than the direct-action rein.

HACKING AND JUMPING

Some riders use training aids such as those described above when hacking as well as schooling. However, in general this cannot be recommended, simply because you are asking a horse to carry himself in a rounded outline for a relatively long time when he probably does not have the muscle development to do so without discomfort.

Never jump a horse under saddle or on the lunge using anything that affects his head carriage, other than a correctly fitted martingale or, under certain circumstances and under expert supervision, a Market Harborough. There is too great a risk of restricting his ability to stretch out his head and neck and causing physical and/or mental pressure that could result in damage or an accident.

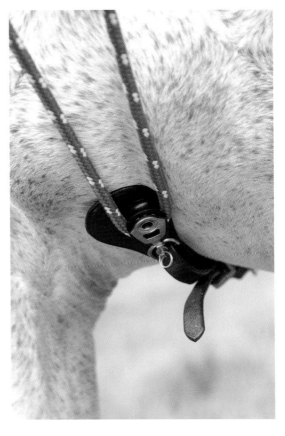

MORE AIDS FOR RIDERS

STRAP SOLUTIONS

We have already looked at how useful a neck strap can be. A balance strap is equally valuable for stabilizing the rider's position and even helping you stay on if a horse bucks. It is simply a strap which fastens to the front D-rings of the saddle; by slipping a finger underneath it or holding the strap and the reins, you will find it easier to sit upright and central in the saddle. You can buy purpose-made balance straps with clips at each end, or use any suitable strap.

MAKING THE BRIDGE

If your horse pulls your reins through your hands during fast work or when jumping a course, you lose balance and control. Jockeys overcome this by bridging their reins but, whilst this is effective when riding horses on the gallops or in a race, it isn't a suitable technique for occasions when you want more flexibility, and it can create too much of a handful for children and others with small hands.

The Mailer bridging rein has been designed to overcome this. By adjusting the bridging loop slightly farther back from where you normally hold the reins, you can ride as normal, but have the immediate security of the bridging position when needed. It is also useful for encouraging the rider to use the reins as a pair, rather than – as often happens – using too much inside rein.

IN CONTACT

Educated riders aim to ride with an elastic contact, maintaining a sympathetic communication with their horse's mouth via the reins and bit without pulling back or setting their hands. Aids to help achieve this include reins with elastic inserts; these have a slight amount of 'give' but do not affect control. Once the rider appreciates the correct feel, it is easier to duplicate it with ordinary reins. Training reins like these can also act as a buffer between the horse's mouth and a novice or uneducated rider's unsteady hands.

LEG AIDS

Symmetry leg-training straps improve the lower leg position of riders who tend to move their legs too far back. By increasing stability, they improve balance and allow you to adopt a correct position until it becomes automatic. **They are not suitable for children**. When using equipment designed to influence rider position, read fitting and safety instructions carefully and use it in a safe, enclosed area to start with.

There are also several designs of stirrup iron designed to help you achieve a secure leg position, which requires toned but not tense muscles. Some of the most popular incorporate hinged foot plates or sides to encourage you to keep your heel slightly lower than your toe. These ease concussion on ankle and knee joints and some riders who suffer from arthritis find they make riding more comfortable.

GOING FORWARD

A wipwop or over-and-under (simply a length of rope knotted to form a handle) can encourage forward movement. Hold the reins in one hand and flick the wipwop over the withers from side to side to touch the horse behind your leg.

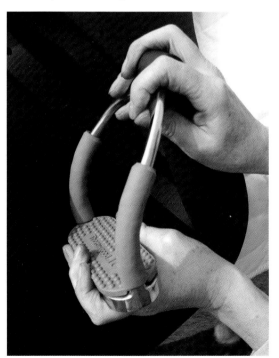

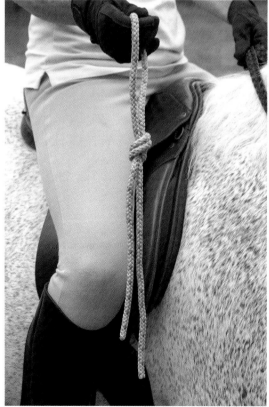

POLE POSITION

You can use poles on the ground as a training aid for any horse or pony, whatever his age or job. They can be incorporated into work under saddle, in hand and on the lunge. Most riders will be familiar with the classic trotting poles: a row of poles on a straight line or a circle set at a distance suitable for the horse's length of stride and used to encourage balance and rhythm. However, there are lots more ways of using poles to enhance the quality of your horse's work and add variety to it. Fit protective boots if needed and, if possible, have a helper to replace any poles that are kicked out of place.

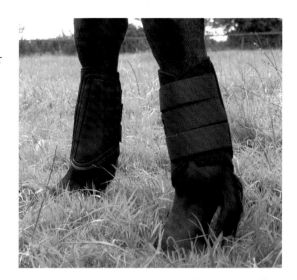

SQUARING THE HALT

If you find it difficult to ride forward and straight into a square halt, build an avenue of poles; this will encourage your horse to keep straight and allow you to focus on riding forward. Place the poles about 3 m apart, starting with four down each side and gradually decreasing the number until you have just two poles at your halt position.

BOX OF POLES

To encourage your horse to step under his body with his inside leg as he turns – and to encourage him to listen to you – make a square of four poles with enough room at each corner to ride through. You can approach in various directions, first in walk and then in trot, riding over poles and through gaps whilst keeping rhythm and bend.

ILPH TECHNIQUES

At the International League for the Protection of Horses' headquarters in Norfolk, in-hand work over poles on the ground is done as part of assessment and rehabilitation programmes. Walking serpentines round poles on the ground shows how the horse uses its limbs and can also highlight stiffness on one side. Walking over four poles on the ground set at a slightly shorter distance than normal encourages a horse to lift his abdominal muscles. If they are set at a slightly longer distance than normal, it helps to free a horse's shoulders.

Work over trotting poles where one or more is raised at alternate ends encourages a horse to flex his joints and think about what he is doing.

ACKNOWLEDGEMENTS

I would like to thank the following manufacturers who supplied equipment for testing and photography: Barnsby; Carol Mailer; EquiAmi; Equilibrium (Symmetry Straps); Libbys Tack (lunge cavesson and Lungie Bungie); Thorowgood (Feeline). Thanks must also go to our Connemaras, Glenn Miller and Hearnesbrook Corbiere, who, thankfully, only charge carrots for their modelling fees.

British Library Cataloguing-in-Publication Data
A catalogue record for this book is available from the British Library

ISBN 978 0 85131 940 7

Published in Great Britain in 2008 by
J. A. Allen an imprint of Robert Hale Ltd.,
Clerkenwell House, 45–47 Clerkenwell Green,
London EC1R 0HT

www.halebooks.com

Design and Typesetting by Paul Saunders
Series editor Jane Lake

Printed by Gutenberg Press Limited, Malta